Gospe...

NEW CENTURY VERSION

INTERNATIONAL CHILDREN'S BIBLE

INTERNATIONAL CHILDREN'S BIBLE – GOSPEL OF MARK
Copyright © 1983, 1988 by Thomas Nelson, Inc. All rights reserved.
This anglicised edition © 1991, 2004 Authentic Media.

The Publisher is pleased hereby to grant permission for the International Children's Bible to be quoted or reprinted without prior written permission with the following qualifications: (1) up to and including one thousand (1,000) verses may be quoted, except: (a) the verses being quoted may not comprise as much as 50% of the work in which it is quoted and (b) the verses quoted may not comprise an entire book of the Bible when quoted.

Quotations from this Bible may be identified in written form with the abbreviation (ICB) (Anglicised Edition) in less formal documents, such as bulletins, newsletters, curricula, media pieces, posters, transparencies and where space is limited.

A proper credit line must appear on the title or copyright page of any work quoting from the International Children's Bible, as follows:

"Scriptures quoted from the International Children's Bible, (Anglicised Edition) copyright © 1991, 2004 by Authentic Media, Milton Keynes, England. Used by permission."

Quotations of more than 1,000 verses, or other permission requests, must be approved by Word Publishing in writing in advance of use.

ISBN: 1-86024-330-4

Published by Authentic Media, 9 Holdom Avenue, Bletchley, Milton Keynes, Bucks, MK1 1QR, UK. All rights reserved.

Book design and production for the publishers by
Bookprint Creative Services, P.O. Box 827, BN21 3YJ, England.
Printed in Great Britain.

Gospel of Mark

John Prepares for Jesus

1 This is the beginning of the Good News about Jesus Christ, the Son of God,[1] ²as the prophet Isaiah wrote:

"I will send my messenger ahead of you.
He will prepare your way."

Malachi 3:1

³"There is a voice of a man who calls out in the desert:
'Prepare the way for the Lord.
Make the road straight for him'."

Isaiah 40:3

⁴John was baptising people in the desert. He preached a baptism of changed hearts and lives for the forgiveness of sins. ⁵All the people from Judea and Jerusalem were going out to John. They told about the sins they had done. Then they were baptised by him in the Jordan River. ⁶John wore clothes made from camel's hair and had a leather belt around his waist. He ate locusts and wild honey. ⁷This is what John preached to the people: "There is one coming later who is greater than I. I am not good enough even to kneel down and untie his sandals. ⁸I baptise you with water.

MARK 1:9

But the one who is coming will baptise you with the Holy Spirit."

Jesus Is Baptised

[9] At that time Jesus came from the town of Nazareth in Galilee to the place where John was. John baptised Jesus in the Jordan River. [10] When Jesus was coming up out of the water, he saw heaven open. The Holy Spirit came down on him like a dove. [11] A voice came from heaven and said: "You are my Son and I love you. I am very pleased with you."

[12] Then the Spirit sent Jesus into the desert alone. [13] He was in the desert 40 days and was there with the wild animals. While he was in the desert, he was tempted by Satan. Then angels came and took care of Jesus.

Jesus Chooses Some Followers

[14] After John was put in prison, Jesus went into Galilee and preached the Good News from God. [15] Jesus said, "The right time has come. The kingdom of God is near. Change your hearts and lives and believe the Good News!"

[16] When Jesus was walking by Lake Galilee, he saw Simon[2] and Simon's brother, Andrew. They were fishermen and were throwing a net into the lake to catch fish. [17] Jesus said to them, "Come and follow me. I will make you fishermen for men." [18] So Simon and Andrew immediately left their nets and followed him.

[19] Jesus continued walking by Lake Galilee. He saw two more brothers, James and John, the sons of Zebedee. They were in their boat, preparing their nets to catch fish. [20] Their father Zebedee and the men who worked for him were in the boat with the brothers. When

Jesus saw the brothers, he called them to come with him. They left their father and followed Jesus.

Jesus Removes an Evil Spirit

21 Jesus and his followers went to Capernaum. On the Sabbath day Jesus went to the synagogue and began to teach. 22 The people there were amazed at his teaching. He did not teach like their teachers of the law. He taught like a person who had authority. 23 While he was in the synagogue, a man was there who had an evil spirit in him. The man shouted, 24 "Jesus of Nazareth! What do you want with us? Did you come to destroy us? I know who you are – God's Holy One!"

25 Jesus said strongly, "Be quiet! Come out of the man!" 26 The evil spirit made the man shake violently. Then the spirit gave a loud cry and came out of him.

27 The people were amazed. They asked each other, "What is happening here? This man is teaching something new. And he teaches with authority. He even gives commands to evil spirits, and they obey him." 28 And the news about Jesus spread quickly everywhere in the area of Galilee.

Jesus Heals Many People

29 Jesus and his followers left the synagogue. They all went at once with James and John to the home of Simon[2] and Andrew. 30 Simon's mother-in-law was sick in bed with a fever. The people there told Jesus about her. 31 So Jesus went to her bed, took her hand, and helped her up. Immediately the fever left her, and she was healed. Then she began serving them.

32 That night, after the sun went down, the people brought to Jesus all who were sick. They also brought those who had demons in them. 33 The whole town

gathered at the door of the house. ³⁴Jesus healed many who had different kinds of sickness. He also forced many demons to leave people. But he would not allow the demons to speak, because they knew who he was.

³⁵Early the next morning, Jesus woke and left the house while it was still dark. He went to a place to be alone and pray. ³⁶Later, Simon and his friends went to look for Jesus. ³⁷They found him and said, "Everyone is looking for you!"

³⁸Jesus answered, "We should go somewhere else, to other towns around here. Then I can preach there too. That is the reason I came." ³⁹So he travelled everywhere in Galilee. He preached in the synagogues and forced demons to leave people.

Jesus Heals a Sick Man

⁴⁰A man who had a harmful skin disease came to Jesus. The man fell to his knees and begged Jesus, "I know that you can heal me if you will."

⁴¹Jesus felt sorry for the man. So he touched him and said, "I want to heal you. Be healed!" ⁴²At once the disease left the man, and he was healed.

⁴³Jesus told the man to go at once. But Jesus warned him strongly, ⁴⁴"Don't tell anyone about what I did for you, but go and show yourself to the priest. And offer a gift to God because you have been healed. Offer the gift that Moses commanded.[3] This will show the people that you are healed." ⁴⁵The man left there, but he told everyone he saw that Jesus had healed him. So the news about Jesus spread. That is the reason Jesus could not enter a town if people saw him. He stayed in places where nobody lived. But people came from all the towns to wherever he was.

Jesus Heals a Paralysed Man

2 A few days later, Jesus came back to Capernaum. The news spread that he was home. ²So many people gathered to hear him preach that the house was full. There was nowhere to stand, not even outside the door. Jesus was teaching them. ³Some people came, bringing a paralysed man to Jesus. Four of them were carrying the paralysed man. ⁴But they could not get to Jesus because of the crowd. So they went to the roof above Jesus and made a hole in the roof. Then they lowered the mat with the paralysed man on it. ⁵Jesus saw that these men had great faith. So he said to the paralysed man, "Young man, your sins are forgiven."

⁶Some of the teachers of the law were sitting there. They saw what Jesus did, and they said to themselves, ⁷"Why does this man say things like that? He is saying things that are against God. Only God can forgive sins."

⁸At once Jesus knew what these teachers of the law were thinking. So he said to them, "Why are you thinking these things? ⁹Which is easier: to tell this paralysed man, 'Your sins are forgiven', or to tell him, 'Stand up. Take your mat and walk'? ¹⁰But I will prove to you that the Son of Man has authority on earth to forgive sins." So Jesus said to the paralysed man, ¹¹"I tell you, stand up. Take your mat and go home." ¹²Immediately the paralysed man stood up. He took his mat and walked out while everyone was watching him.

The people were amazed and praised God. They said, "We have never seen anything like this!"

¹³Jesus went to the lake again. A crowd followed him there, and he taught them. ¹⁴While he was walking beside the lake, he saw a tax collector named Levi son of Alphaeus. Levi was sitting in the tax office. Jesus said to him, "Follow me". And Levi stood up and followed Jesus.

MARK 2:15

[15]Later that day, Jesus ate at Levi's house. There were many tax collectors and "sinners" eating there with Jesus and his followers. Many people like this followed Jesus. [16]The teachers of the law who were Pharisees saw Jesus eating with the tax collectors and "sinners". They asked his followers, "Why does he eat with tax collectors and 'sinners'?"

[17]Jesus heard this and said to them, "Healthy people don't need a doctor. It is the sick who need a doctor. I did not come to invite good people. I came to invite sinners."

Jesus' Followers Are Criticised

[18]One day the followers of John[4] and the Pharisees were giving up eating.[5] Some people came to Jesus and said, "John's followers and the followers of the Pharisees give up eating, but your followers don't. Why?"

[19]Jesus answered, "When there is a wedding, the friends of the bridegroom are not sad while he is with them. They do not give up eating while the bridegroom is still there. [20]But the time will come when the bridegroom will leave them. Then the friends will be sad and will give up eating.

[21]"When a person sews a patch over a hole on an old coat, he never uses a piece of cloth that is not yet shrunk. If he does, the patch will shrink and pull away from the coat. Then the hole will be worse. [22]Also, no one ever pours new wine into old leather bags for holding wine. If he does, the new wine will break the bags, and the wine will be ruined along with the bags for the wine. People always put new wine into new leather bags."

Jesus Is Lord of the Sabbath

²³On the Sabbath day, Jesus was walking through some grainfields. His followers were with him and picked some grain to eat. ²⁴The Pharisees saw this and said to Jesus, "Why are your followers doing what is not lawful on the Sabbath?"

²⁵Jesus answered, "You have read what David did when he and those with him were hungry and needed food. ²⁶It was during the time of Abiathar the high priest. David went into God's house and ate the bread that was made holy for God. The law of Moses says that only priests may eat that bread. But David also gave some of the bread to those who were with him."

²⁷Then Jesus said to the Pharisees, "The Sabbath day was made to help people. They were not made to be ruled by the Sabbath day. ²⁸The Son of Man is Lord even of the Sabbath."

Jesus Heals a Man's Crippled Hand

3 Another time when Jesus went into a synagogue, a man with a crippled hand was there. ²Some people there wanted to see Jesus do something wrong so they could accuse him. They watched him closely to see if he would heal the man on the Sabbath day.

³Jesus said to the man with the crippled hand, "Stand up here in front of everyone."

⁴Then Jesus asked the people, "Which is right on the Sabbath day: to do good, or to do evil? Is it right to save a life or to destroy one?" But they said nothing to answer him.

⁵Jesus was angry as he looked at the people. But he felt very sad because they were stubborn. Then he said to the man, "Let me see your hand." The man put his hand out for Jesus, and it was healed. ⁶Then the

MARK 3:7

Pharisees left and began making plans with the Herodians[6] about a way to kill Jesus.

Many People Follow Jesus

⁷Jesus left with his followers for the lake. A large crowd from Galilee followed him. ⁸Also many people came from Judea, from Jerusalem, from Idumea, from the lands across the Jordan River, and from the area of Tyre and Sidon. They came because they had heard about all the things Jesus was doing. ⁹Jesus saw the crowds. So he told his followers to get a boat ready for him. He wanted the boat so that the many people would not crowd themselves against him. ¹⁰He had healed many people. So all the sick were pushing toward him to touch him. ¹¹Some had evil spirits in them. When the evil spirits saw Jesus, they fell down before him and shouted, "You are the Son of God!" ¹²But Jesus strongly commanded the spirits not to tell who he was.

Jesus Chooses His 12 Apostles

¹³Then Jesus went up on a hill and called some men to come to him. These were the men Jesus wanted, and they went up to him. ¹⁴Jesus chose 12 men and called them apostles. He wanted these 12 to be with him, and he wanted to send them to other places to preach. ¹⁵He also wanted them to have the power to force demons out of people. ¹⁶These are the 12 men he chose: Simon (Jesus gave him the name Peter); ¹⁷James and John, the sons of Zebedee (Jesus gave them the name Boanerges, which means "Sons of Thunder"); ¹⁸Andrew, Philip, Bartholomew, Matthew, Thomas, James the son of Alphaeus, Thaddaeus, Simon the Zealot, ¹⁹and Judas Iscariot. Judas is the one who gave Jesus to his enemies.

People Say Jesus Has a Devil

²⁰Then Jesus went back home. But again a crowd gathered. There were so many people that Jesus and his followers could not eat. ²¹His family heard about all these things. They went to get him because people were saying that Jesus was out of his mind.

²²And the teachers of the law from Jerusalem were saying, "Beelzebul is living inside him! He uses power from the ruler of demons to force demons out."

²³So Jesus called the people together and used stories to teach them. He said, "Satan will not force his own demons out of people. ²⁴A kingdom that fights against itself cannot continue, ²⁵and a family that is divided cannot continue. ²⁶And if Satan is against himself and fights against his own people, then he cannot continue. And that is the end of Satan. ²⁷If a person wants to enter a strong man's house and steal his things, first he must tie up the strong man. Then the thief can steal the things from the strong man's house. ²⁸I tell you the truth. All sins that people do can be forgiven. And all the bad things people say against God can be forgiven. ²⁹But any person who says bad things against the Holy Spirit will never be forgiven. He is guilty of a sin that continues for ever."

³⁰Jesus said this because the teachers of the law said that Jesus had an evil spirit inside him.

Jesus' True Family

³¹Then Jesus' mother and brothers arrived. They stood outside and sent someone in to tell him to come out. ³²Many people were sitting around Jesus. They said to him, "Your mother and brothers are waiting for you outside."

³³Jesus asked, "Who is my mother? Who are my

brothers?" ³⁴Then Jesus looked at those sitting around him. He said, "Here are my mother and my brothers! ³⁵My true brother and sister and mother are those who do the things God wants."

A Story About Planting Seed

4 Another time Jesus began teaching by the lake. A great crowd gathered around him. So he got into a boat and went out on the lake. All the people stayed on the shore close to the water. ²Jesus used many stories to teach them. He said, ³"Listen! A farmer went out to plant his seed. ⁴While the farmer was planting, some seed fell by the road. The birds came and ate all that seed. ⁵Some seed fell on rocky ground where there wasn't much soil. The seed grew very fast there because the ground was not deep. ⁶But when the sun rose, the plants withered. The plants died because they did not have deep roots. ⁷Some other seed fell among thorny weeds. The weeds grew and choked the good plants. So those plants did not make grain. ⁸Some other seed fell on good ground. In the good ground, the seed began to grow. It grew and made a crop of grain. Some plants made 30 times more grain, some 60 times more grain, and some 100 times more grain."

⁹Then Jesus said, "You people who hear me, listen!"

Jesus Tells Why He Used Stories

¹⁰Later, when Jesus was alone, the 12 apostles and others around him asked him about the stories.

¹¹Jesus said, "Only you can know the secret truth about the kingdom of God. But to other people I tell everything by using stories. ¹²I do this so that:

'They will look and look, but they will not learn.
They will listen and listen, but they will not
 understand.
If they did learn and understand, they would
 come back to me and be forgiven'."

Isaiah 6:9–10

Jesus Explains the Seed Story

[13] Then Jesus said to the followers, "Do you understand this story? If you don't, then how will you understand any story? [14] The farmer is like a person who plants God's teaching in people. [15] Sometimes the teaching falls on the road. This is like some people. They hear the teaching of God. But Satan quickly comes and takes away the teaching that was planted in them. [16] Others are like the seed planted on rocky ground. They hear the teaching and quickly accept it with joy. [17] But they don't allow the teaching to go deep into their lives. They keep it only a short time. When trouble or persecution comes because of the teaching, they quickly give up. [18] Others are like the seed planted among the thorny weeds. They hear the teaching. [19] But then other things come into their lives: worries, the love of money, and wanting all kinds of other things. These things stop the teaching from growing. So that teaching does not produce fruit[7] in their lives. [20] Others are like the seed planted in the good ground. They hear the teaching and accept it. Then they grow and produce fruit – sometimes 30 times more, sometimes 60 times more, and sometimes 100 times more."

Use What You Have

[21] Then Jesus said to them, "Do you hide a lamp under a bowl or under a bed? No! You put the lamp on a lamp-

MARK 4:22

stand. ²²Everything that is hidden will be made clear. Every secret thing will be made known. ²³You people who hear me, listen!

²⁴"Think carefully about the things you hear. The way you give to others is the way God will give to you. But God will give you more than you give. ²⁵The person who has something will be given more. But the person who does not have much, even what he has will be taken from him."

Jesus Uses a Story About Seed

²⁶Then Jesus said, "The kingdom of God is like a man who plants seed in the ground. ²⁷The seed comes up and grows night and day. It doesn't matter whether the man is asleep or awake; the seed still grows. The man does not know how it grows. ²⁸Without any help, the earth produces grain. First the plant grows, then the head, and then all the grain in the head. ²⁹When the grain is ready, the man cuts it. This is the harvest time."

A Story About Mustard Seed

³⁰Then Jesus said, "How can I show you what the kingdom of God is like? What story can I use to explain it? ³¹The kingdom of God is like a mustard seed. The mustard seed is the smallest seed you plant in the ground. ³²But when you plant this seed, it grows and becomes the largest of all garden plants. It produces large branches. Even the wild birds can make nests in it and be protected from the sun."

³³Jesus used many stories like these to teach them. He taught them all that they could understand. ³⁴He always used stories to teach them. But when he and his followers were alone together, Jesus explained everything to them.

Jesus Stops a Storm

³⁵That evening, Jesus said to his followers, "Come with me across the lake." ³⁶He and the followers left the people there. They went in the boat that Jesus was already sitting in. There were also other boats with them. ³⁷A very strong wind came up on the lake. The waves began coming over the sides and into the boat. It was almost full of water. ³⁸Jesus was at the back of the boat, sleeping with his head on a pillow. The followers went to him and woke him. They said, "Teacher, do you care about us? We will drown!"

³⁹Jesus stood up and commanded the wind and the waves to stop. He said, "Quick! Be still!" Then the wind stopped, and the lake became calm.

⁴⁰Jesus said to his followers, "Why are you afraid? Do you still have no faith?"

⁴¹The followers were very afraid and asked each other, "What kind of man is this? Even the wind and the waves obey him!"

A Man with Demons Inside Him

5 Jesus and his followers went across the lake to the region of the Gerasene people. ²When Jesus got out of the boat, a man came to him from the caves where dead people were buried. This man, who lived in the caves, had an evil spirit living in him. ³No one could tie him up, not even with a chain. ⁴Many times people had used chains to tie the man's hands and feet. But he always broke the chains off. No one was strong enough to control him. ⁵Day and night he would wander around the burial caves and on the hills, screaming and cutting himself with stones. ⁶While Jesus was still far away, the man saw him. He ran to Jesus and knelt down before him. ⁷⁻⁸Jesus said to the man, "You evil spirit, come out of that man."

MARK 5:9

But the man shouted in a loud voice, "What do you want with me, Jesus, Son of the Most High God? I beg you, promise God that you will not punish me!"

⁹Then Jesus asked the man, "What is your name?"

The man answered, "My name is Legion,[8] because I have many spirits in me." ¹⁰The man begged Jesus again and again not to send the spirits out of that area.

¹¹A large herd of pigs was eating on a hill near there. ¹²The evil spirits begged Jesus, "Send us to the pigs. Let us go into them." ¹³So Jesus allowed them to do this. The evil spirits left the man and went into the pigs. Then the herd of pigs rushed down the hill into the lake and were drowned. There were about 2,000 pigs in that herd.

¹⁴The men who took care of the pigs ran away. They went to the town and to the countryside, telling everyone about this. So people went out to see what had happened. ¹⁵They came to Jesus and saw the man who had had the many evil spirits. The man was sitting there, clothed and in his right mind. The people were frightened. ¹⁶Some people were there who saw what Jesus had done. They told the others what had happened to the man who had the demons living in him. And they also told about the pigs. ¹⁷Then the people began to beg Jesus to leave their area.

¹⁸Jesus was getting ready to leave in the boat. The man who was freed from the demons begged to go with him.

¹⁹But Jesus would not allow the man to go. Jesus said, "Go home to your family and friends. Tell them how much the Lord has done for you and how he has had mercy on you." ²⁰So the man left and told the people in the Ten Towns[9] about the great things Jesus had done for him. All the people were amazed.

Jesus Gives Life to a Dead Girl and Heals a Sick Woman

[21] Jesus went in the boat back to the other side of the lake. There, a large crowd gathered around him. [22] A ruler from the synagogue, named Jairus, came to that place. Jairus saw Jesus and bowed before him. [23] The ruler begged Jesus again and again. He said, "My little daughter is dying. Please come and put your hands on her. Then she will be healed and will live." [24] So Jesus went with the ruler, and many people followed Jesus. They were pushing very close around him.

[25] A woman was there who had been bleeding for the past 12 years. [26] She had suffered very much. Many doctors had tried to help her. She had spent all the money she had, but she was not improving. She was getting worse. [27] When the woman heard about Jesus, she followed him with the people and touched his coat. [28] The woman thought, "If I can even touch his coat, that will be enough to heal me." [29] When she touched his coat, her bleeding stopped. She could feel in her body that she was healed.

[30] At once Jesus felt power go out from him. So he stopped and turned around. Then he asked, "Who touched my clothes?"

[31] The followers said, "There are so many people pushing against you! And you ask, 'Who touched me?'"

[32] But Jesus continued looking around to see who had touched him. [33] The woman knew that she was healed. So she came and bowed at Jesus' feet. Shaking with fear, she told him the whole story. [34] Jesus said to the woman, "Dear woman, you are made well because you believed. Go in peace. You will have no more suffering."

[35] Jesus was still speaking to her when some men came from the house of Jairus, the synagogue ruler. The men

said, "Your daughter is dead. There is now no need to bother the teacher."

³⁶But Jesus paid no attention to what the men said. He said to the synagogue ruler, "Don't be afraid; only believe."

³⁷Jesus let only Peter, James, and John the brother of James go with him to Jairus's house. ³⁸They came to the house of the synagogue ruler, and Jesus found many people were crying loudly. There was much confusion. ³⁹Jesus entered the house and said to the people, "Why are you crying and making so much noise? This child is not dead. She is only asleep." ⁴⁰But they only laughed at Jesus. He told all the people to leave. Then he went into the room where the child was. He took the child's father and mother and his three followers into the room with him. ⁴¹Then he took hold of the girl's hand and said to her, "Talitha, koum!" (This means, "Little girl, I tell you to stand up!") ⁴²The girl stood right up and began walking. (She was 12 years old.) The father and mother and the followers were amazed. ⁴³Jesus gave the father and mother strict orders not to tell people about this. Then he told them to give the girl some food.

Jesus Goes to His Home Town

6 Jesus left there and went back to his home town. His followers went with him. ²On the Sabbath day he taught in the synagogue. Many people heard him and were amazed. They said, "Where did this man get these teachings? What is this wisdom that has been given to him? And where did he get the power to work miracles? ³He is only the carpenter. His mother is Mary. He is the brother of James, Joseph, Judas, and Simon. And his sisters are here with us." The people did not accept Jesus.

⁴Jesus said to them, "Other people give honour to a prophet. But in his own town with his own people and in his own home, a prophet does not receive honour." ⁵Jesus was not able to work many miracles there. The only miracles he did were to heal some sick people by putting his hands on them. ⁶Jesus was amazed that they had no faith.

Then Jesus went to other villages in that area and taught. ⁷He called the 12 followers together and sent them out in groups of two. He gave them authority over evil spirits. ⁸This is what Jesus told them: "Take nothing for your trip except a walking stick. Take no bread, no bag, and no money in your pockets. ⁹Wear sandals, and take only the clothes you are wearing. ¹⁰When you enter a house, stay there until you leave that place. ¹¹If any town refuses to accept you or its people refuse to listen to you, then leave that town. Shake its dust off your feet.[10] This will be a warning to them."

¹²The followers went out and preached to the people to change their hearts and lives. ¹³The followers forced many demons out and poured olive oil on many sick people and healed them.

How John the Baptist Was Killed

¹⁴King Herod heard about Jesus, because Jesus was now well-known. Some people said, "He is John the Baptist. He is risen from death. That is the reason he can work these miracles."

¹⁵Others said, "He is Elijah."[11]

Other people said, "Jesus is a prophet. He is like the prophets who lived long ago."

¹⁶Herod heard all these things about Jesus. He said, "I killed John by cutting off his head. Now he has been raised from death!"

MARK 6:17

[17] Herod himself had ordered his soldiers to arrest John, and John was put in prison. Herod did this to please his wife, Herodias. Herodias was the wife of Philip, Herod's brother. But then Herod married her. [18] John told Herod that it was not lawful for him to be married to his brother's wife. [19] So Herodias hated John and wanted to kill him. But she could not because of Herod. [20] Herod was afraid to kill John because he knew John was a good and holy man. So Herod protected John. Also, Herod enjoyed listening to John preach. But John's preaching always bothered him.

[21] Then the perfect time came for Herodias to cause John's death. It happened on Herod's birthday. Herod gave a dinner party for the most important government leaders, the commanders of his army, and the most important people in Galilee. [22] The daughter of Herodias came to the party and danced. When she danced, Herod and the people eating with him were very pleased.

So King Herod said to the girl, "I will give you anything you want." [23] He promised her, "Anything you ask for I will give to you. I will even give you half of my kingdom."

[24] The girl went to her mother and asked, "What should I ask the king to give me?"

Her mother answered, "Ask for the head of John the Baptist."

[25] Quickly the girl went back to the king. She said to him, "Please give me the head of John the Baptist. Bring it to me now on a platter."

[26] The king was very sad. But he had promised to give the girl anything she wanted. And the people eating there with him had heard his promise. So Herod could not refuse what she asked. [27] Immediately the king sent

a soldier to bring John's head. The soldier went and cut off John's head in the prison ²⁸and brought it back on a platter. He gave it to the girl, and the girl gave it to her mother. ²⁹John's followers heard about what happened. So they came and got John's body and put it in a tomb.

More than 5,000 People Fed

³⁰The apostles that Jesus had sent out to preach returned. They gathered around him and told him about all the things they had done and taught. ³¹Crowds of people were coming and going. Jesus and his followers did not even have time to eat. He said to them, "Come with me. We will go to a quiet place to be alone. There we will get some rest."

³²So they went in a boat alone to a place where there were no people. ³³But many people saw them leave and recognised them. So people from all the towns ran to the place where Jesus was going. They got there before Jesus arrived. ³⁴When he landed, he saw a great crowd waiting. Jesus felt sorry for them, because they were like sheep without a shepherd. So he taught them many things.

³⁵It was now late in the day. Jesus' followers came to him and said, "No one lives in this place. And it is already very late. ³⁶Send the people away. They need to go to the farms and towns around here to buy some food to eat."

³⁷But Jesus answered, "You give them food to eat."

They said to him, "We can't buy enough bread to feed all these people! We would all have to work a month to earn enough money to buy that much bread!"

³⁸Jesus asked them, "How many loaves of bread do you have now? Go and see."

When they found out, they came to him and said, "We have five loaves and two fish."

MARK 6:39

[39] Then Jesus said to the followers, "Tell all the people to sit in groups on the green grass." [40] So all the people sat in groups. They sat in groups of 50 or groups of 100. [41] Jesus took the five loaves and two fish. He looked up to heaven and thanked God for the bread. He divided the bread and gave it to his followers for them to give to the people. Then he divided the two fish among them all. [42] All the people ate and were satisfied. [43] The followers filled 12 baskets with the pieces of bread and fish that were not eaten. [44] There were about 5,000 men there who ate.

Jesus Walks on the Water

[45] Then Jesus told his followers to get into the boat and go to Bethsaida on the other side of the lake. Jesus said that he would come later. He stayed there to tell the people they could go home. [46] After sending them away, he went into the hills to pray.

[47] That night, the boat was in the middle of the lake. Jesus was alone on the land. [48] He saw the followers working hard to row the boat because the wind was blowing against them. At some time between three and six o'clock in the morning, Jesus came to them, walking on the water. He continued walking until he was almost past the boat. [49] But when his followers saw him walking on the water, they thought he was a ghost and cried out. [50] They all saw him and were terrified. But Jesus spoke to them and said, "Have courage! It is I! Do not be afraid." [51] Then he got into the boat with them. And the wind became calm. The followers were greatly amazed. [52] They had seen Jesus make more bread from the five loaves. But they did not understand what it meant. Their minds were closed.

[53] When they had crossed the lake, they came to shore

at Gennesaret. They tied the boat there. [54]When they got out of the boat, the people saw Jesus and immediately recognised him. [55]They ran to tell others everywhere in that area that Jesus was there. They brought sick people on mats to every place Jesus went. [56]Jesus went into towns and cities and farms around that area. And everywhere he went, the people brought the sick to the marketplaces. They begged him to let them just touch the edge of his coat. And all who touched him were healed.

Obey God's Law Not Men's

7 Some Pharisees and some teachers of the law came from Jerusalem. They gathered around Jesus. [2]They saw that some of Jesus' followers ate food with hands that were not clean. ("Not clean" means that they did not wash their hands in the way the Pharisees said people must. [3]The Pharisees and all the Jews never eat before washing their hands in this special way. They do this to follow the teaching given to them by their great people who lived before them. [4]And when the Jews buy something in the market, they never eat it until they have washed it in a special way. They also follow other rules of their great people who lived before them. They follow rules about the washing of cups, pitchers, and pots.)

[5]The Pharisees and the teachers of the law said to Jesus, "Your followers don't follow the rules given to us by our great people who lived before us. Your followers eat their food with hands that are not clean. Why do they do this?"

[6]Jesus answered, "You are all hypocrites! Isaiah was right when he spoke about you. Isaiah wrote,

MARK 7:7

'These people show honour to me with words.
But their hearts are far from me.
⁷Their worship of me is worthless.
The things they teach are nothing but human
   rules they have memorised'.

Isaiah 29:13

⁸You have stopped following the commands of God. Now you only follow the teachings of men."

⁹Then Jesus said to them: "You think you are clever! You ignore the commands of God so that you can follow your own teachings! ¹⁰Moses said, 'Honour your father and mother'.[12] Then Moses also said, 'Anyone who says cruel things to his father or mother must be put to death'.[13] ¹¹But you teach that a person can say to his father or mother, 'I have something I could use to help you. But I will not use it for you. I will give it to God'. ¹²You are telling that person that he does not have to do anything for his father or mother. ¹³So you are teaching that it is not important to do what God said. You think that it is more important to follow your own rules, which you teach people. And you do many things like that."

¹⁴Jesus called the people to him again. He said, "Every person should listen to me and understand what I am saying. ¹⁵There is nothing a person puts into his body that makes him unclean. A person is made unclean by the things that come out of him."[16][14]

¹⁷When Jesus left the people and went inside, his followers asked him about this story. ¹⁸Jesus said, "Do you still have trouble understanding? Surely you know that nothing that enters a man from the outside can make him unclean. ¹⁹Food does not go into a person's mind. Food goes into his stomach. Then that food goes out of

his body." (When Jesus said this, he meant that there is no food that is unclean for people to eat.)

²⁰And Jesus said, "The things that come out of a man are the things that make him unclean. ²¹All these evil things begin inside a person, in his mind: evil thoughts, sexual sins, stealing, murder, adultery, ²²selfishness, doing bad things to other people, lying, doing sinful things, jealousy, saying bad things about people, pride, and foolish living. ²³All these evil things come from within a person. These things make a person unclean."

Jesus Helps a Non-Jewish Woman

²⁴Jesus left that place and went to the area around Tyre. He went into a house and did not want anyone to know he was there. But Jesus could not stay hidden. ²⁵A woman heard that he was there. Her little daughter had an evil spirit in her. So the woman quickly came to Jesus and fell at his feet. ²⁶She was not Jewish. She was Greek, born in Phoenicia, in Syria. She begged Jesus to force the demon out of her daughter.

²⁷Jesus told the woman: "It is not right to take the children's bread and give it to the dogs. First let the children eat all they want."

²⁸She answered, "That is true, Lord. But the dogs under the table can eat the pieces of food that the children don't eat."

²⁹Then Jesus said, "That is a very good answer. You may go. The demon has left your daughter."

³⁰The woman went home and found her daughter lying in bed. The demon was gone.

Jesus Heals a Deaf Man

³¹Then Jesus left the area around Tyre. He went through Sidon to Lake Galilee, to the area of the Ten

MARK 7:32

Towns.[9] ³²While he was there, some people brought a man to him. This man was deaf and could not talk. The people begged Jesus to put his hand on the man to heal him.

³³Jesus led the man away from the crowd, to be alone with him. Jesus put his fingers in the man's ears. Then Jesus spat and touched the man's tongue. ³⁴Jesus looked up to heaven and took a deep breath. He said to the man, "Ephphatha!" (This means, "Be opened".) ³⁵When Jesus did this, the man was able to hear. He was also able to use his tongue, and he spoke clearly.

³⁶Jesus commanded the people not to tell anyone about what happened. But the more he commanded them, the more they told about it. ³⁷They were really amazed. They said, "Jesus does everything well. He makes the deaf hear! And those who can't talk – Jesus makes them able to speak."

More than 4,000 People Fed

8 Another time there was a great crowd with Jesus. They had nothing to eat. So Jesus called his followers to him. He said, ²"I feel sorry for these people. They have been with me for three days, and now they have nothing to eat. ³I cannot send them home hungry. If they leave without eating, they will faint on the way home. Some of them live a long way from here."

⁴Jesus' followers answered, "But we are far away from any towns. Where can we get enough bread to feed all these people?"

⁵Jesus asked, "How many loaves of bread do you have?"

They answered, "We have seven loaves."

⁶Jesus told the people to sit on the ground. Then he took the seven loaves and gave thanks to God. Jesus

divided the bread and gave the pieces to his followers. He told them to pass out the bread to the people, and they did so. ⁷The followers also had a few small fish. Jesus gave thanks for the fish and told his followers to give the fish to the people. ⁸All the people ate and were satisfied. Then the followers filled seven baskets with the pieces of food that were not eaten. ⁹There were about 4,000 men who ate. After they had eaten, Jesus told them to go home. ¹⁰Then he went in a boat with his followers to the area of Dalmanutha.

The Leaders Ask for a Miracle

¹¹The Pharisees came to Jesus and asked him questions. They wanted to trap him. So they asked Jesus to do a miracle to show that he was from God. ¹²Jesus sighed deeply. He said, "Why do you people ask for a miracle as proof? I tell you the truth. No miracle will be given to you." ¹³Then Jesus left the Pharisees. He went in the boat to the other side of the lake.

Guard Against Wrong Teachings

¹⁴The followers had only one loaf of bread with them in the boat. They had forgotten to bring more bread. ¹⁵Jesus warned them, "Be careful! Guard against the yeast of the Pharisees and the yeast of Herod."

¹⁶Among themselves, his disciples discussed the meaning of this. They said, "He said this because we have no bread."

¹⁷Jesus knew what his followers were talking about. So he asked them, "Why are you talking about having no bread? You still don't see or understand? Are your minds closed? ¹⁸You have eyes, but you don't really see. You have ears, but you don't really listen. Remember what I did before, when we did not have

MARK 8:19

enough bread? ¹⁹I divided five loaves of bread for 5,000 people. Remember how many baskets you filled with pieces of food that were not eaten?"

They answered, "We filled 12 baskets."

²⁰"And remember that I divided seven loaves of bread for 4,000 people. Remember how many baskets you filled with pieces of food that were not eaten?"

They answered, "We filled seven baskets."

²¹Then Jesus said to them, "You remember these things I did, but you still don't understand?"

Jesus Heals a Blind Man

²²Jesus and his followers came to Bethsaida. Some people brought a blind man to Jesus and begged him to touch the man. ²³So Jesus took the blind man's hand and led him out of the village. Then he spat on the man's eyes. He put his hands on the blind man and asked, "Can you see now?"

²⁴The man looked up and said, "Yes, I see people, but they look like trees walking around."

²⁵Again Jesus put his hands on the man's eyes. Then the man opened his eyes wide. His eyes were healed, and he was able to see everything clearly. ²⁶Jesus told him to go home, saying, "Don't go into the town."

Peter Says Jesus Is the Christ

²⁷Jesus and his followers went to the towns around Caesarea Philippi. While they were travelling, Jesus asked them, "Who do people say I am?"

²⁸They answered, "Some people say you are John the Baptist. Others say you are Elijah.[11] And others say that you are one of the prophets."

²⁹Then Jesus asked, "Who do you say I am?"

Peter answered, "You are the Christ."

³⁰Jesus ordered his followers, "Don't tell anyone who I am."

³¹Then Jesus began to teach them that the Son of Man must suffer many things. He taught that the Son of Man would not be accepted by the older Jewish leaders, the leading priests, and the teachers of the law. He taught that the Son of Man must be killed and then rise from death after three days. ³²Jesus told them plainly what would happen. Then Peter took Jesus aside and began to criticise him. ³³But Jesus turned and looked at his followers. Then he criticised Peter and said, "Go away from me, Satan![15] You don't care about the things of God. You care only about things men think are important."

³⁴Then Jesus called the crowd to him, along with his followers. He said, "If anyone wants to follow me, he must say 'no' to the things he wants. He must be willing to die on a cross, and he must follow me. ³⁵Whoever wants to save his life will give up true life. But whoever gives up his life for me and for the Good News will have true life for ever. ³⁶It is worth nothing for a person to have the whole world, if he loses his soul. ³⁷A person could never pay enough to buy back his soul. ³⁸The people who live now are living in a sinful and evil time. If anyone is ashamed of me and my teaching, then I will be ashamed of him. I will be ashamed of him when I come with the glory of my Father and the holy angels."

9 Then Jesus said to the people, "I tell you the truth. Some of you standing here will see the kingdom of God come with power before you die."

Jesus with Moses and Elijah

²Six days later Jesus took Peter, James, and John and went up on a high mountain. They were all alone there.

While these followers watched, Jesus was changed. ³His clothes became shining white, whiter than any person could make them. ⁴Then two men appeared, talking with Jesus. The men were Moses and Elijah.[16]

⁵Peter said to Jesus, "Teacher, it is good that we are here. We will put three tents here – one for you, one for Moses, and one for Elijah." ⁶Peter did not know what to say, because he and the others were so frightened.

⁷Then a cloud came and covered them. A voice came from the cloud. The voice said, "This is my Son, and I love him. Obey him!"

⁸Then Peter, James, and John looked around, but they saw only Jesus there alone with them.

⁹As Jesus and his followers were walking back down the mountain, he commanded them, "Don't tell anyone about the things you saw on the mountain. Wait till the Son of Man rises from death. Then you may tell."

¹⁰So the followers obeyed Jesus and said nothing about what they had seen. But they discussed what Jesus meant about rising from death.

¹¹They asked Jesus, "Why do the teachers of the law say that Elijah must come first?"

¹²Jesus answered, "They are right to say that Elijah must come first. Elijah makes all things the way they should be. But why does the Scripture say that the Son of Man will suffer much and that people will treat him as if he were nothing? ¹³I tell you that Elijah has already come. And people did to him whatever they wanted to do. The Scriptures said this would happen to him."

Jesus Heals a Sick Boy

¹⁴Then Jesus, Peter, James, and John went to the other followers. They saw a great crowd around them. The

teachers of the law were arguing with them. ¹⁵But when the crowd saw Jesus, they were surprised and ran to welcome him.

¹⁶Jesus asked, "What are you arguing about with the teachers of the law?"

¹⁷A man answered, "Teacher, I brought my son to you. He has a spirit from the devil in him. This spirit stops him from talking. ¹⁸The spirit attacks him and throws him on the ground. My son foams at the mouth, grinds his teeth, and becomes very stiff. I asked your followers to force the evil spirit out, but they couldn't."

¹⁹Jesus answered, "You people don't believe! How long must I stay with you? How long must I go on being patient with you? Bring the boy to me!"

²⁰So the followers brought him to Jesus. As soon as the evil spirit saw Jesus, it attacked the boy. He fell down and rolled on the ground, foaming from his mouth.

²¹Jesus asked the boy's father, "How long has this been happening?"

The father answered, "Since he was very young. ²²The spirit often throws him into a fire or into water to kill him. If you can do anything for him, please have pity on us and help us."

²³Jesus said to the father, "You said, 'If you can!' All things are possible for him who believes."

²⁴Immediately the father cried out, "I do believe! Help me to believe more!"

²⁵Jesus saw that a crowd was running there to see what was happening. So he spoke to the evil spirit, saying, "You deaf and dumb spirit—I command you to come out of this boy and never enter him again!"

²⁶The evil spirit screamed and caused the boy to fall on the ground again. Then the spirit came out. The boy

MARK 9:27

looked as if he were dead. And many people said, "He is dead!" ²⁷But Jesus took hold of the boy's hand and helped him to stand up.

²⁸Jesus went into the house. His followers were alone with him there. They said, "Why couldn't we force that evil spirit out?"

²⁹Jesus answered, "That kind of spirit can only be forced out by prayer."

Jesus Talks About His Death

³⁰Then Jesus and his followers left that place and went through Galilee. Jesus did not want anyone to know where he was ³¹because he wanted to teach his followers alone. He said to them, "The Son of Man will be given to men who will kill him. After three days, he will rise from death." ³²But the followers did not understand what Jesus meant. And they were afraid to ask.

Who Is the Greatest?

³³Jesus and his followers went to Capernaum and went into a house there. Then Jesus said to them, "What were you arguing about on the road?" ³⁴But the followers did not answer, because their argument on the road was about which one of them was the greatest.

³⁵Jesus sat down and called the 12 apostles to him. He said, "If anyone wants to be the most important, then he must be last of all and servant of all."

³⁶Then Jesus took a small child and had him stand among them. He took the child in his arms and said, ³⁷"If anyone accepts children like these in my name, then he is also accepting me. And if he accepts me, then he is also accepting the One who sent me."

Anyone Not Against Us Is For Us

38Then John said, "Teacher, we saw a man using your name to force demons out of a person. We told him to stop, because he does not belong to our group."

39Jesus said, "Don't stop him. Anyone who uses my name to do powerful things will not say evil things about me. 40He who is not against us is with us. 41I tell you the truth. If anyone helps you by giving you a drink of water because you belong to the Christ, then he will truly get his reward.

42"If one of these little children believes in me, and someone causes that child to sin, then it will be very bad for him. It would be better for him to have a large stone tied around his neck and be drowned in the sea. 43If your hand causes you to sin, cut it off. It is better for you to lose part of your body but have life for ever. That is much better than to have two hands and go to hell. In that place the fire never goes out. 44[17] 45If your foot causes you to sin, cut it off. It is better for you to lose part of your body but have life for ever. That is much better than to have two feet and be thrown into hell. 46[17] 47If your eye causes you to sin, take it out. It is better for you to have only one eye but have life for ever. That is much better than to have two eyes and be thrown into hell. 48In hell the worm does not die; the fire is never stopped. 49Every person will be salted with fire.

50"Salt is good. But if the salt loses its salty taste, then you cannot make it salty again. So, be full of goodness. And have peace with each other."

Jesus Teaches About Divorce

10 Then Jesus left that place. He went into the area of Judea and across the Jordan River. Again, crowds came to him. And Jesus taught them as he always did.

MARK 10:2

²Some Pharisees came to Jesus and tried to trick him. They asked, "Is it right for a man to divorce his wife?"

³Jesus answered, "What did Moses command you to do?"

⁴They said, "Moses allowed a man to write out divorce papers and send her away."[18]

⁵Jesus said, "Moses wrote that command for you because you refused to accept God's teaching. ⁶But when God made the world, 'he made them male and female'.[19] ⁷'So a man will leave his father and mother and be united with his wife. ⁸And the two people will become one body'.[20] So the people are not two, but one. ⁹God has joined the two people together. So no one should separate them."

¹⁰Later, the followers and Jesus were in the house. They asked Jesus again about the question of divorce. ¹¹He answered, "Anyone who divorces his wife and marries another woman is guilty of adultery against her. ¹²And the woman who divorces her husband and marries another man is also guilty of adultery."

Jesus Accepts Children

¹³Some people brought their small children to Jesus so he could touch them. But his followers told the people to stop bringing their children to him. ¹⁴When Jesus saw this, he was displeased. He said to them, "Let the little children come to me. Don't stop them. The kingdom of God belongs to people who are like these little children. ¹⁵I tell you the truth. You must accept the kingdom of God as a little child accepts things, or you will never enter it." ¹⁶Then Jesus took the children in his arms. He put his hands on them and blessed them.

A Rich Young Man's Question

[17] Jesus started to leave, but a man ran to him and fell on his knees before Jesus. The man asked, "Good teacher, what must I do to get the life that never ends?"

[18] Jesus answered, "Why do you call me good? No one is good except God alone. [19] You know the commands: 'You must not murder anyone. You must not be guilty of adultery. You must not steal. You must not tell lies about your neighbour in court. You must not cheat. Honour your father and mother'."[21]

[20] The man said, "Teacher, I have obeyed all these commands since I was a boy."

[21] Jesus looked straight at the man and loved him. Jesus said, "There is still one more thing you need to do. Go and sell everything you have, and give the money to the poor. You will have a reward in heaven. Then come and follow me."

[22] He was very sad to hear Jesus say this, and he left. The man was sad because he was very rich.

[23] Then Jesus looked at his followers and said, "How hard it will be for those who are rich to enter the kingdom of God!"

[24] The followers were amazed at what Jesus said. But he said again, "My children, it is very hard to enter the kingdom of God! [25] And it will be very hard for a rich person to enter the kingdom of God. It would be easier for a camel to go through the eye of a needle!"

[26] The followers were even more amazed and said to each other, "Then who can be saved?"

[27] Jesus looked straight at them and said, "This is something that men cannot do. But God can do it. God can do all things."

[28] Peter said to Jesus, "We left everything to follow you!"

MARK 10:29

²⁹Jesus said, "I tell you the truth. Everyone who has left his home, brothers, sisters, mother, father, children, or fields for me and for the Good News ³⁰will get a hundred times more than he left. Here in this world he will have more homes, brothers, sisters, mothers, children, and fields. And with those things, he will also suffer for his belief. But in the age that is coming he will have life for ever. ³¹Many who have the highest place now will have the lowest place in the future. And those who have the lowest place now will have the highest place in the future."

Jesus Talks About His Own Death

³²Jesus and the people with him were on the road to Jerusalem. Jesus was leading the way. The followers were amazed, but those who followed behind them were afraid. Jesus took the 12 apostles aside and talked with them alone. He told them what would happen in Jerusalem. ³³He said, "We are going to Jerusalem. The Son of Man will be given to the leading priests and teachers of the law. They will say that he must die. They will give him to the non-Jewish people, ³⁴who will laugh at him and spit on him. They will beat him with whips and kill him. But on the third day after his death, he will rise to life again."

Two Followers Ask Jesus a Favour

³⁵Then James and John, sons of Zebedee, came to Jesus. They said, "Teacher, we want to ask you to do something for us."

³⁶Jesus asked, "What do you want me to do for you?"

³⁷They answered, "You will have glory in your kingdom. Let one of us sit at your right, and let one of us sit at your left."

[38]Jesus said, "You don't understand what you are asking. Can you drink the cup that I must drink? And can you be baptised with the same kind of baptism that I must have?"[22]

[39]They answered, "Yes, we can!"

Jesus said to them, "You will drink the same cup that I will drink. And you will be baptised with the same baptism that I must have. [40]But I cannot choose who will sit at my right or my left. These places are for those for whom they are prepared."

[41]The ten followers heard this. They began to be angry with James and John.

[42]Jesus called all the followers together. He said, "The non-Jewish people have men they call rulers. You know that those rulers love to show their power over the people. And their important leaders love to use all their authority. [43]But it should not be that way among you. If one of you wants to become great, then he must serve you like a servant. [44]If one of you wants to become the most important, then he must serve all of you like a slave. [45]In the same way, the Son of Man did not come to be served. He came to serve. The Son of Man came to give his life to save many people."

Jesus Heals a Blind Man

[46]Then they came to the town of Jericho. As Jesus was leaving there with his followers and a large crowd, a blind beggar named Bartimaeus (son of Timaeus) was sitting by the road. [47]He heard that Jesus from Nazareth was walking by. The blind man cried out, "Jesus, Son of David, please help me!"

[48]Many people scolded the blind man and told him to be quiet. But he shouted more and more, "Son of David, please help me!"

MARK 10:49

[49] Jesus stopped and said, "Tell the man to come here."

So they called the blind man. They said, "Cheer up! Get to your feet. Jesus is calling you." [50] The blind man stood up quickly. He left his coat there and went to Jesus.

[51] Jesus asked him, "What do you want me to do for you?"

The blind man answered, "Teacher, I want to see again."

[52] Jesus said, "Go. You are healed because you believed." At once the man was able to see again, and he followed Jesus on the road.

Jesus Enters Jerusalem as a King

11 Jesus and his followers were coming closer to Jerusalem. They came to the towns of Bethphage and Bethany near the Mount of Olives. There Jesus sent two of his followers. [2] He said to them, "Go to the town you see there. When you enter it, you will find a colt tied which no one has ever ridden. Untie it and bring it here to me. [3] If anyone asks you why you are doing this, tell him, 'The Master needs the colt. He will send it back soon'."

[4] The followers went into the town. They found a colt tied in the street near the door of a house, and they untied it. [5] Some people were standing there and asked, "What are you doing? Why are you untying the colt?" [6] The followers answered the way Jesus told them to answer, and the people let them take the colt.

[7] The followers brought the colt to Jesus. They put their coats on the colt, and Jesus sat on it. [8] Many people spread their coats on the road. Others cut branches in the fields and spread the branches on the road. [9] Some

of the people were walking ahead of Jesus. Others were following him. All of them were shouting.

> "Praise[23] God!
> God bless the One who comes in the name of the Lord!
>
> Psalm 118:26
>
> [10]God bless the kingdom of our father David!
> That kingdom is coming!
> Praise to God in heaven!"

[11]Jesus entered Jerusalem and went into the Temple. When he had looked at everything, and since it was already late, he went out to Bethany with the 12 apostles.

[12]The next day as Jesus was leaving Bethany, he was hungry. [13]He saw a fig tree in leaf. So he went to the tree to see if it had any figs on it. But he found no figs, only leaves. It was not the right season for figs to grow. [14]So Jesus said to the tree, "May no one ever eat fruit from you again." Jesus' followers heard him say this.

Jesus Goes to the Temple

[15]Jesus returned to Jerusalem and went into the Temple. He began to throw out those who were buying and selling things there. He overturned the tables that belonged to the men who were exchanging different kinds of money. And he turned over the benches of the men who were selling doves. [16]Jesus refused to allow anyone to carry goods through the Temple courts. [17]Then Jesus taught the people. He said, "It is written in the Scriptures, 'My Temple will be a house where people from all nations will pray'.[24] But

MARK 11:18

you are changing God's house into a 'hideout for robbers'."[25]

[18]The leading priests and the teachers of the law heard all this. They began trying to find a way to kill Jesus. They were afraid of him because all the people were amazed at his teaching. [19]That night, Jesus and his followers left the city.

The Power of Faith

[20]The next morning, Jesus was passing by with his followers. They saw the fig tree, and it was dry and dead, even to the roots. [21]Peter remembered the tree and said to Jesus, "Teacher, look! Yesterday, you cursed the fig tree. Now it is dry and dead!"

[22]Jesus answered, "Have faith in God. [23]I tell you the truth. You can say to this mountain, 'Go, mountain, fall into the sea'. And if you have no doubts in your mind and believe that the thing you say will happen, then God will do it for you. [24]So I tell you to ask for things in prayer. And if you believe that you have received those things, then they will be yours. [25]When you are praying, and you remember that you are angry with another person about something, then forgive him. If you do this, then your Father in heaven will also forgive your sins."[26][26]

Leaders Doubt Jesus' Authority

[27]Jesus and his followers went again to Jerusalem. Jesus was walking in the Temple. The leading priests, the teachers of the law, and the older Jewish leaders came to him. [28]They said to him, "Tell us! What authority do you have to do these things? Who gave you this authority?"

[29]Jesus answered, "I will ask you one question. You

answer it. Then I will tell you whose authority I use to do these things. ³⁰Tell me: when John baptised people, was that from God or from man? Answer me!"

³¹They argued about Jesus' question. They said to each other, "If we answer, 'John's baptism was from God', then Jesus will say, 'Then why didn't you believe John?' ³²But if we say, 'From man', then the people will be against us." (These leaders were afraid of the people. All the people believed that John was a prophet.)

³³So the leaders answered Jesus, "We don't know."

Jesus said, "Then I will not tell you what authority I use to do these things."

God Sends His Son

12 Jesus used stories to teach the people. He said, "A man planted a vineyard. He put a wall around it and dug a hole for a winepress. Then he built a tower. He leased the vineyard to some farmers and left for a trip. ²Later, it was time for the grapes to be picked. So the man sent a servant to the farmers to get his share of the grapes. ³But the farmers grabbed the servant and beat him. They sent him away with nothing. ⁴Then the man sent another servant. They hit him on the head and showed no respect for him. ⁵So the man sent another servant. They killed this servant. The man sent many other servants. The farmers beat some of them and killed others.

⁶"The man had one person left to send, his son whom he loved. He sent him last of all, saying, 'The farmers will respect my son'.

⁷"But they said to each other, 'This is the owner's son. This vineyard will be his. If we kill him, then it will be ours'. ⁸So they took the son, killed him, and threw him out of the vineyard.

MARK 12:9

⁹"So what will the man who owns the vineyard do? He will go to the vineyard and kill those farmers. Then he will give the vineyard to other farmers. ¹⁰Surely you have read this Scripture:

> 'The stone that the builders did not want became the cornerstone.
> ¹¹The Lord did this, and it is wonderful to us'."
>
> Psalm 118:22–23

¹²The Jewish leaders knew that the story was about them. So they wanted to find a way to arrest Jesus, but they were afraid of the people. So the leaders left him and went away.

The Leaders Try to Trap Jesus

¹³Later, the Jewish leaders sent some Pharisees and some men from the group called Herodians[6] to Jesus. They wanted to catch Jesus saying something wrong. ¹⁴They came to him and said, "Teacher, we know that you are an honest man. You are not afraid of what other people think about you. All men are the same to you. And you teach the truth about God's way. Tell us: is it right to pay taxes to Caesar? Should we pay them, or not?"

¹⁵But Jesus knew what these men were really trying to do. He said, "Why are you trying to trap me? Bring me a silver coin. Let me see it." ¹⁶They gave Jesus a coin, and he asked, "Whose picture is on the coin? And whose name is written on it?"

They answered, "Caesar's."

¹⁷Then Jesus said to them, "Give to Caesar the things that are Caesar's. And give to God the things that are God's." The men were amazed at what Jesus said.

Sadducees Try to Trick Jesus

[18] Then some Sadducees came to Jesus. (Sadducees believe that no person will rise from death.) The Sadducees asked Jesus a question. [19] They said, "Teacher, Moses wrote that a man's brother might die. He leaves a wife but no children. Then that man must marry the widow and have children for the dead brother. [20] There were seven brothers. The first brother married but died. He had no children. [21] So the second brother married the widow. But he also died and had no children. The same thing happened with the third brother. [22] All seven brothers married her and died. None of the brothers had any children. The woman was last to die. [23] But all seven brothers had married her. So at the time people rise from death, whose wife will the woman be?"

[24] Jesus answered, "Why did you make this mistake? Is it because you don't know what the Scriptures say? Or is it because you don't know about the power of God? [25] When people rise from death, there will be no marriage. People will not be married to each other but will be like angels in heaven. [26] Surely you have read what God said about people rising from death. In the book in which Moses wrote about the burning bush,[27] it says that God told Moses this: 'I am the God of Abraham, the God of Isaac, and the God of Jacob'.[28] [27] God is the God of living people, not dead people. You Sadducees are wrong!"

The Most Important Command

[28] One of the teachers of the law came to Jesus. He heard Jesus arguing with the Sadducees and the Pharisees. He saw that Jesus gave good answers to their questions. So he asked Jesus, "Which of the commands is most important?"

²⁹Jesus answered, "The most important command is this: 'Listen, people of Israel! The Lord our God, he is the only Lord. ³⁰Love the Lord your God. Love him with all your heart, all your soul, all your mind, and all your strength'.[29] ³¹The second most important command is this: 'Love your neighbour as you love yourself'.[30] These two commands are the most important commands."

³²The man answered, "That was a good answer, Teacher. You were right when you said these things. God is the only Lord, and there is no other God besides him. ³³A person must love God with all his heart, all his mind, and all his strength. And he must love his neighbour as he loves himself. These commands are more important than all the animals and sacrifices we offer to God."

³⁴Jesus saw that the man answered him wisely. So Jesus said to him, "You are close to the kingdom of God." And after that, no one was brave enough to ask Jesus any more questions.

³⁵Jesus was teaching in the Temple. He asked, "Why do the teachers of the law say that the Christ is the son of David? ³⁶David himself, speaking by the Holy Spirit, said:

'The Lord said to my Lord:
Sit by me at my right side, until I put your
    enemies under your control'.

Psalm 110:1

³⁷David himself calls the Christ 'Lord'. So how can the Christ be David's son?" The large crowd listened to Jesus with pleasure.

³⁸Jesus continued teaching. He said, "Beware of the teachers of the law. They like to walk around wearing

clothes that look important. And they love people to show respect to them in the marketplaces. ³⁹They love to have the most important seats in the synagogues. And they love to have the most important seats at the feasts. ⁴⁰They cheat widows and steal their homes. Then they try to make themselves look good by saying long prayers. God will punish these people terribly."

True Giving
⁴¹Jesus sat near the Temple money box where people put their gifts. He watched the people put in their money. Many rich people gave large sums of money. ⁴²Then a poor widow came and gave two very small copper coins. These coins were not worth even a penny.

⁴³Jesus called his followers to him. He said, "I tell you the truth. This poor widow gave only two small coins. But she really gave more than all those rich people. ⁴⁴The rich have plenty; they gave only what they did not need. This woman is very poor, but she gave all she had. And she needed that money to help her live."

The Temple Will Be Destroyed
13 Jesus was leaving the Temple. One of his followers said to him, "Look, Teacher! This Temple has beautiful buildings with very big stones."

²Jesus said, "Do you see all these great buildings? Every stone will be thrown to the ground. Not one stone will be left on another."

³Later, Jesus was sitting on the Mount of Olives. He was alone with Peter, James, John, and Andrew. They could all see the Temple. They asked Jesus, ⁴"Tell us, when will all these things happen? And what will show us that the time has come for them to happen?"

⁵Jesus said to them: "Be careful that no one fools you. ⁶Many people will come and use my name. They will say, 'I am the One'. And they will fool many. ⁷You will hear about wars and stories of wars that are coming. But don't be afraid. These things must happen before the end comes. ⁸Nations will fight against other nations. Kingdoms will fight against other kingdoms. There will be times when there is no food for people to eat. And there will be earthquakes in different places. These things are like the first pains when something new is about to be born.

⁹"You must be careful. People will arrest you and take you to court. They will beat you in their synagogues. You will be forced to stand before kings and governors, to tell them about me. This will happen to you because you follow me. ¹⁰But before these things happen, the Good News must be told to all people. ¹¹When you are arrested and judged, don't worry about what you should say. Say the things God gives you to say at that time. It will not really be you speaking. It will be the Holy Spirit.

¹²"Brothers will turn against their own brothers and give them over to be killed. Fathers will turn against their own children and give them over to be killed. Children will fight against their own parents and cause their parents to be killed. ¹³All people will hate you because you follow me. But the person who continues to be strong until the end will be saved.

¹⁴"You will see 'the horrible thing that destroys'.[31] You will see this thing standing in the place where it should not be." (You who read this should understand what it means.) "At that time, the people in Judea should run away to the mountains. ¹⁵If a person is on the roof[32] of his house, he must not go down to take anything out of his house. ¹⁶If a person is in the field, he

must not go back to get his coat. [17]At that time, it will be hard for women who are pregnant or have nursing babies. [18]Pray that these things will not happen in winter. [19]This is because those days will be full of trouble. There will be more trouble than there has ever been since the beginning, when God made the world. And nothing as bad will ever happen again. [20]God has decided to make that terrible time short. If that time were not made short, then no one would go on living. But God will make that time short to help his special people whom he has chosen. [21]At that time, someone might say to you, 'Look, there is the Christ!' Or another person might say, 'There he is!' But don't believe them. [22]False Christs and false prophets will come and perform great wonders and miracles. They will do these things to the people God has chosen. They will do these things to try to fool them, if that is possible. [23]So be careful. For I have warned you about all this before it happens.

[24]"During the days after this trouble comes,

'The sun will grow dark.
And the moon will not give its light.
[25]The stars will fall from the sky.
And everything in the sky will be changed'.
Isaiah 13:10; 34:4

[26]"Then people will see the Son of Man coming in clouds with great power and glory. [27]The Son of Man will send his angels all around the earth. They will gather his chosen people from every part of the earth.

[28]"The fig tree teaches us a lesson: when its branches become green and soft, and new leaves begin to grow, then you know that summer is near. [29]So also when you

see all these things happening, then you will know that the time is near, ready to come. ³⁰I tell you the truth. All these things will happen while the people of this time are still living. ³¹The whole world, earth and sky, will be destroyed, but the words I have said will never be destroyed.

³²"No one knows when that day or time will be. The Son and the angels in heaven don't know. Only the Father knows. ³³Be careful! Always be ready! You don't know when that time will be. ³⁴It is like a man who goes on a trip. He leaves his house and lets his servants take care of it. He gives each servant a special job to do. One servant has the work of guarding the door. The man tells this servant always to be watchful. This is what I am now telling you. ³⁵You must always be ready. You don't know when the owner of the house will come back. He might come in the evening, or at midnight, or in the early morning, or when the sun rises. ³⁶He might come back quickly. If you are always ready, then he will not find you sleeping. ³⁷I tell you this, and I say this to everyone: 'Be ready!'"

The Plan to Kill Jesus

14 It was now only two days before the Passover and the Feast of Unleavened Bread. The leading priests and teachers of the law were trying to find a way to use some trick to arrest Jesus and kill him. ²But they said, "We must not do it during the feast. The people might cause a riot."

A Woman with Perfume for Jesus

³Jesus was in Bethany. He was at dinner in the house of Simon, who had a harmful skin disease. While Jesus was there, a woman came to him. She had an alabaster

jar filled with very expensive perfume, made of pure nard. The woman opened the jar and poured the perfume on Jesus' head.

⁴Some of those who were there saw this and became angry. They complained to each other, saying, "Why waste that perfume? ⁵It was worth a full year's work. It could be sold, and the money could be given to the poor." They spoke to the woman sharply.

⁶Jesus said, "Don't bother the woman. Why are you troubling her? She did a beautiful thing for me. ⁷You will always have the poor with you. You can help them whenever you want. But you will not always have me. ⁸This woman did the only thing she could do for me. She poured perfume on my body. She did this before I die to prepare me for burial. ⁹I tell you the truth. The Good News will be told to people in all the world. And in every place it is preached, what this woman has done will be told. And people will remember her."

Judas Becomes an Enemy of Jesus

¹⁰One of the 12 followers, Judas Iscariot, went to talk to the leading priests. Judas offered to give Jesus to them. ¹¹The leading priests were pleased about this. They promised to pay Judas money. So he waited for the best time to give Jesus to them.

Jesus Eats the Passover Feast

¹²It was now the first day of the Feast of Unleavened Bread. This was a time when the Jews always sacrificed the Passover lambs. Jesus' followers came to him. They said, "We will go and prepare everything for the Passover Feast. Where do you want to eat the feast?"

¹³Jesus sent two of his followers and said to them, "Go into the city. A man carrying a jar of water will meet you.

MARK 14:14

Follow him. ¹⁴He will go into a house. Tell the owner of the house, 'The Teacher asks that you show us the room where he and his followers can eat the Passover Feast'. ¹⁵The owner will show you a large room upstairs. This room is ready. Prepare the food for us there."

¹⁶So the followers left and went into the city. Everything happened as Jesus had said. So they prepared the Passover Feast.

¹⁷In the evening, Jesus went to that house with the 12. ¹⁸While they were all eating, Jesus said, "I tell you the truth. One of you will give me to my enemies – one of you eating with me now."

¹⁹The followers were very sad to hear this. Each one said to Jesus, "I am not the one, am I?"

²⁰Jesus answered, "The man who is against me is one of the 12. He is the one who dips his bread into the bowl with me. ²¹The Son of Man must go and die. The Scriptures say this will happen. But how terrible it will be for the person who gives the Son of Man to be killed. It would be better for that person if he had never been born."

The Lord's Supper

²²While they were eating, Jesus took some bread. He thanked God for it and broke it. Then he gave it to his followers and said, "Take it. This bread is my body."

²³Then Jesus took a cup. He thanked God for it and gave it to the followers. All the followers drank from the cup.

²⁴Then Jesus said, "This is my blood which begins the new agreement that God makes with his people. This blood is poured out for many. ²⁵I tell you the truth. I will not drink of this fruit of the vine[33] again until that day when I drink it new in the kingdom of God."

²⁶They sang a hymn and went out to the Mount of Olives.

Jesus' Followers Will All Leave Him.

²⁷Then Jesus told the followers,

> "You will all lose your faith in me. It is written in the Scriptures:
> 'I will kill the shepherd, and the sheep will scatter'.
>
> *Zechariah 13:7*

²⁸But after I rise from death, I will go ahead of you into Galilee."

²⁹Peter said, "All the other followers may lose their faith. But I will not."

³⁰Jesus answered, "I tell you the truth. Tonight you will say you don't know me. You will say this three times before the cock crows twice."

³¹But Peter answered strongly, "I will never say that I don't know you! I will even die with you!" And all the other followers said the same thing.

Jesus Prays Alone

³²Jesus and his followers went to a place called Gethsemane. He said to his followers, "Sit here while I pray." ³³Jesus told Peter, James, and John to come with him. Then Jesus began to be very sad and troubled. ³⁴He said to them, "I am full of sorrow. My heart is breaking with sadness. Stay here and watch."

³⁵Jesus walked a little further away from them. Then he fell on the ground and prayed. He prayed that, if possible, he would not have this time of suffering. ³⁶He prayed, "Abba,[34] Father! You can do all things. Let me

MARK 14:37

not have this cup[35] of suffering. But do what you want, not what I want."

⁣³⁷Then Jesus went back to his followers. He found them asleep. He said to Peter, "Simon, why are you sleeping? You could not stay awake with me for one hour? ³⁸Stay awake and pray that you will not be tempted. Your spirit wants to do what is right, but your body is weak."

³⁹Again Jesus went away and prayed the same thing. ⁴⁰Then he went back to the followers. Again he found them asleep because their eyes were very heavy. And they did not know what to say to Jesus.

⁴¹After Jesus prayed a third time, he went back to his followers. He said to them, "You are still sleeping and resting? That's enough! The time has come for the Son of Man to be given to sinful people. ⁴²Get up! We must go. Here comes the man who has turned against me."

Jesus Is Arrested

⁴³While Jesus was still speaking, Judas came up. Judas was one of the 12 followers. He had many people with him. They were sent from the leading priests, the teachers of the law, and the older Jewish leaders. Those with Judas had swords and clubs.

⁴⁴Judas had planned a signal for them. He had said, "The man I kiss is Jesus. Arrest him and guard him while you lead him away." ⁴⁵So Judas went to Jesus and said, "Teacher!" and kissed him. ⁴⁶Then the men grabbed Jesus and arrested him. ⁴⁷One of the followers standing near drew his sword. He struck the servant of the high priest with the sword and cut off his ear.

⁴⁸Then Jesus said, "You came to get me with swords and clubs as if I were a criminal. ⁴⁹Every day I was with you teaching in the Temple. You did not arrest me there. But all these things have happened to make the

Scriptures come true." ⁵⁰Then all of Jesus' followers left him and ran away.

⁵¹A young man, wearing only a linen cloth, was following Jesus. The people also grabbed him. ⁵²But the cloth he was wearing came off, and he ran away naked.

Jesus Before the Leaders

⁵³The people who arrested Jesus led him to the house of the high priest. All the leading priests, the older Jewish leaders, and the teachers of the law were gathered there. ⁵⁴Peter followed far behind and entered the courtyard of the high priest's house. There he sat with the guards, warming himself by the fire.

⁵⁵The leading priests and all the Jewish council tried to find something that Jesus had done wrong so they could kill him. But the council could find no proof against him. ⁵⁶Many people came and told false things about him. But all said different things – none of them agreed.

⁵⁷Then some men stood up and lied about Jesus. They said, ⁵⁸"We heard this man say, 'I will destroy this Temple that men made. And three days later, I will build another Temple – a Temple not made by men'." ⁵⁹But even the things these men said did not agree.

⁶⁰Then the high priest stood before them and said to Jesus. "Aren't you going to answer the charges these men bring against you?" ⁶¹But Jesus said nothing. He did not answer.

The high priest asked Jesus another question: "Are you the Christ, the Son of the blessed God?"

⁶²Jesus answered, "I am. And in the future you will see the Son of Man sitting at the right side of the Powerful One. And you will see the Son of Man coming on clouds in the sky."

MARK 14:63

⁶³When the high priest heard this, he was very angry. He tore his clothes and said, "We don't need any more witnesses! ⁶⁴You all heard him say these things against God. What do you think?"

They all said that Jesus was guilty and should be killed. ⁶⁵Some of the people there spat at Jesus. They covered his eyes and hit him with their fists. They said, "Prove that you are a prophet!" Then the guards led Jesus away and beat him.

Peter Says He Doesn't Know Jesus

⁶⁶Peter was still in the courtyard when a servant girl of the high priest came there. ⁶⁷She saw Peter warming himself at the fire. She looked closely at him.

Then the girl said, "You were with Jesus, that man from Nazareth."

⁶⁸But Peter said that he was never with Jesus. He said, "I don't know or understand what you are talking about." Then Peter left and went toward the entrance of the courtyard.[36]

⁶⁹The servant girl saw Peter there. Again she said to the people who were standing there, "This man is one of those who followed Jesus." ⁷⁰Again Peter said that it was not true.

A short time later, some people were standing near Peter. They said, "We know you are one of those who followed Jesus. You are from Galilee, too."

⁷¹Then Peter began to curse. He said, "I swear that I don't know this man you're talking about!"

⁷²As soon as Peter said this, the cock crowed the second time. Then Peter remembered what Jesus had told him: "Before the cock crows twice, you will say three times that you don't know me." Then Peter was very sad and began to cry.

Pilate Questions Jesus

15 Very early in the morning, the leading priests, the older Jewish leaders, the teachers of the law, and all the Jewish council decided what to do with Jesus. They tied him, led him away, and turned him over to Pilate, the governor.

[2] Pilate asked Jesus, "Are you the king of Jews?"

Jesus answered, "Yes, I am."

[3] The leading priests accused Jesus of many things. [4] So Pilate asked Jesus another question. He said, "You can see that these people are accusing you of many things. Why don't you answer?"

[5] But Jesus still said nothing. Pilate was very surprised at this.

Pilate Tries to Free Jesus

[6] Every year at the Passover time the governor would free one person from prison. He would free any person the people wanted him to free. [7] At that time, there was a man named Barabbas in prison. He was a rebel and had committed murder during a riot. [8] The crowd came to Pilate and asked him to free a prisoner as he always did.

[9] Pilate asked them, "Do you want me to free the king of the Jews?" [10] Pilate knew that the leading priests had given Jesus to him because they were jealous of Jesus. [11] And the leading priests had persuaded the people to ask Pilate to free Barabbas, not Jesus.

[12] Pilate asked the crowd again, "So what should I do with this man you call the king of the Jews?"

[13] They shouted, "Kill him on a cross!"

[14] Pilate asked, "Why? What wrong has he done?"

But they shouted louder and louder, "Kill him on a cross!"

MARK 15:15

¹⁵Pilate wanted to please the crowd. So he freed Barabbas for them. And Pilate told the soldiers to beat Jesus with whips. Then he gave Jesus to the soldiers to be killed on a cross.

¹⁶Pilate's soldiers took Jesus into the governor's palace (called the Praetorium). They called all the other soldiers together. ¹⁷They put a purple robe on Jesus. Then they used thorny branches to make a crown. They put it on his head. ¹⁸Then they called out to him, "Hail, King of the Jews!" ¹⁹The soldiers beat Jesus on the head many times with a stick. They also spat on him. Then they made fun of him by bowing on their knees and worshipping him. ²⁰After they had finished making fun of him, the soldiers took off the purple robe and put his own clothes on him again. Then they led Jesus out of the palace to be killed on a cross.

Jesus Is Killed on a Cross

²¹There was a man from Cyrene coming from the fields to the city. The man was Simon, the father of Alexander and Rufus. The soldiers forced Simon to carry the cross for Jesus. ²²They led Jesus to the place called Golgotha. (Golgotha means the Place of the Skull.) ²³At Golgotha the soldiers tried to give Jesus wine to drink. This wine was mixed with myrrh. But he refused to drink it. ²⁴The soldiers nailed Jesus to a cross. Then they divided his clothes among themselves. They threw lots to decide which clothes each soldier would get.

²⁵It was nine o'clock in the morning when they nailed Jesus to the cross. ²⁶There was a sign with the charge against Jesus written on it. The sign read: "THE KING OF THE JEWS". ²⁷They also put two robbers on crosses beside Jesus, one on the right, and the other on the left. ²⁸[37] ²⁹People walked by and insulted Jesus. They shook

their heads, saying, "You said you could destroy the Temple and build it again in three days. [30]So save yourself! Come down from that cross!"

[31]The leading priests and the teachers of the law were also there. They made fun of Jesus just as the other people did. They said among themselves, "He saved other people, but he can't save himself. [32]If he is really the Christ, the king of Israel, then let him come down from the cross now. We will see this, and then we will believe in him." The robbers who were being killed on the crosses beside Jesus also insulted him.

Jesus Dies

[33]At noon the whole country became dark. This darkness lasted for three hours. [34]At three o'clock Jesus cried in a loud voice, "Eloi, Eloi, lama sabachthani." This means, "My God, my God, why have you left me alone?"

[35]Some of the people standing there heard this. They said, "Listen! He is calling Elijah."

[36]One man there ran and got a sponge. He filled the sponge with vinegar and tied it to a stick. Then he used the stick to give the sponge to Jesus to drink from it. The man said, "We should wait now and see if Elijah will come to take him down from the cross."

[37]Then Jesus cried in a loud voice and died.

[38]When Jesus died, the curtain in the Temple[38] split into two pieces. The tear started at the top and tore all the way to the bottom. [39]The army officer that was standing there before the cross saw what happened when Jesus died. The officer said, "This man really was the Son of God!"

[40]Some women were standing at a distance from the cross, watching. Some of these women were Mary Magdalene, Salome, and Mary the mother of James and

MARK 15:41

Joseph (James was her youngest son.) ⁴¹These were the women who followed Jesus in Galilee and cared for him. Many other women were also there who had come with Jesus to Jerusalem.

Jesus Is Buried

⁴²This was Preparation Day. (That means the day before the Sabbath day.) It was becoming dark. ⁴³A man named Joseph from Arimathea was brave enough to go to Pilate and ask for Jesus' body. Joseph was an important member of the Jewish council. He was one of the people who wanted the kingdom of God to come. ⁴⁴Pilate wondered if Jesus was already dead. Pilate called the army officer who guarded Jesus and asked him if Jesus had already died. ⁴⁵The officer told Pilate that he was dead. So Pilate told Joseph he could have the body. ⁴⁶Joseph bought some linen cloth, took the body down from the cross and wrapped it in the linen. He put the body in a tomb that was cut in a wall of rock. Then he closed the tomb by rolling a very large stone to cover the entrance. ⁴⁷And Mary Magdalene and Mary the mother of Joseph saw the place where Jesus was laid.

Jesus Rises from Death

16 The day after the Sabbath day, Mary Magdalene, Mary the mother of James, and Salome bought some sweet-smelling spices to put on Jesus' body. ²Very early on that day, the first day of the week, the women were on their way to the tomb. It was soon after sunrise. ³They said to each other, "There is a large stone covering the entrance of the tomb. Who will move the stone for us?"

⁴Then the women looked and saw that the stone had

already been moved. The stone was very large, but it had been moved away from the entrance. ⁵The women entered the tomb and saw a young man wearing a white robe. He was sitting on the right side, and the women were afraid.

⁶But the man said, "Don't be afraid. You are looking for Jesus from Nazareth, the one who was killed on a cross. He has risen from death. He is not here. Look, here is the place they laid him. ⁷Now go and tell his followers and Peter, 'Jesus is going into Galilee. He will be there before you. You will see him there as he told you before'."

⁸The women were confused and shaking with fear. They left the tomb and ran away. They did not tell anyone about what happened, because they were afraid.[39]

Some Followers See Jesus

⁹Jesus rose from death early on the first day of the week. He showed himself first to Mary Magdalene. Once in the past, he had forced seven demons to leave Mary. ¹⁰After Mary saw Jesus, she went and told his followers. They were very sad and were crying. ¹¹But Mary told them that Jesus was alive. She said that she had seen him, but the followers did not believe her.

¹²Later, Jesus showed himself to two of his followers while they were walking in the country. But Jesus did not look the same as before. ¹³These followers went back to the others and told them what had happened. Again, the followers did not believe them.

Jesus Talks to the Apostles

¹⁴Later Jesus showed himself to the 11 followers while they were eating. He criticised them because they had

MARK 16:15

little faith. They were stubborn and refused to believe those who had seen him after he had risen from death.

[15] Jesus said to the followers, "Go everywhere in the world. Tell the Good News to everyone. [16] Anyone who believes and is baptised will be saved. But he who does not believe will be judged guilty. [17] And those who believe will be able to do these things as proof: they will use my name to force demons out of people. They will speak in languages[40] they never learned. [18] They will pick up snakes without being hurt. And they will drink poison without being hurt. They will touch the sick, and the sick will be healed."

[19] After the Lord Jesus said these things to the followers, he was carried up into heaven. There, Jesus sat at the right side of God. [20] The followers went everywhere in the world and told the Good News to people. And the Lord helped them. The Lord proved that the Good News they told was true by giving them power to work miracles.

Notes

[1] Some Greek copies omit these words.

[2] Simon's other name was Peter.

[3] Read about this in Leviticus 14:1–32.

[4] John the Baptist who preached to the Jews about Christ's coming (Mark 1:4–8).

[5] This is called "fasting". The people would give up eating for a special time of prayer and worship to God. It was also done to show sadness.

[6] A political group that followed Herod and his family.

[7] To produce fruit means to have in your life the good things God wants.

[8] Means very many. A legion was about 5,000 men in the Roman army.

[9] In Greek, called "Decapolis". It was an area east of Lake Galilee that once had ten main towns.

[10] A warning. It showed that they had finished talking to these people.

[11] A man who spoke for God. He lived hundreds of years before Christ.

Notes

[12] Quotation from Exodus 20:12; Deuteronomy 5:16.

[13] Quotation from Exodus 21:17.

[14] Some Greek copies add verse 16: "You people who hear me, listen!"

[15] Name for the devil meaning "the enemy". Jesus means that Peter was talking like Satan.

[16] Two of the most important Jewish leaders in the past. *See also* note 11.

[17] Some Greek copies of Mark add verses 44 and 46, which are the same as verse 48.

[18] Quotation from Deuteronomy 24:1.

[19] Quotation from Genesis 1:27.

[20] Quotation from Genesis 2:24.

[21] Quotation from Exodus 20:12–16; Deuteronomy 5:16–20.

[22] Jesus was asking if they could suffer the same terrible things that would happen to him.

[23] Literally, "Hosanna", a Hebrew word used at first in praying to God for help, but at this time it was probably a shout of joy used in praising God or his Messiah.

[24] Quotation from Isaiah 56:7.

[25] Quotation from Jeremiah 7:11.

[26] Some early Greek copies add verse 26: "But if you don't forgive other people, then your Father in heaven will not forgive your sins."

Notes

[27] Read Exodus 3:1–12 in the Old Testament.

[28] Quotation from Exodus 3:6.

[29] Quotation from Deuteronomy 6:4–5.

[30] 'Love . . . yourself'. Quotation from Leviticus 19:18.

[31] Mentioned in Daniel 9:27; 12:11 (cf. Daniel 11:31).

[32] In Bible times houses were built with flat roofs. The roof was used for drying things such as flax and fruit. It was also used as an extra room, as a place for worship and as a place to sleep in the summer.

[33] Product of the grapevine; this may also be translated "wine".

[34] Name that a child called his father.

[35] Jesus is talking about the bad things that will happen to him. Accepting these things will be very hard, like drinking a cup of something that tastes very bitter.

[36] Many Greek copies add: "And the cock crowed."

[37] Some Greek copies add verse 28: "And the Scripture came true that says, 'They put him with criminals'."

[38] A curtain divided the Most Holy Place from the other part of the Temple. That was the special building in Jerusalem where God commanded the Jews to worship him.

[39] Some early Greek copies end the book with verse 8.

[40] This can also be translated "tongues".